Kingdom Curriculum for Kids

Title ID: 1-5028253-7-6
ISBN-13: 978-1502825377

© 2015 REIGN Worldwide, Inc.

REIGN Worldwide Publications
P.O. Box 1083
Keller, Texas 76244

All Scripture quotations, unless noted otherwise, are from the Holy Bible, *King James Version.*

Scripture quotations marked (AMP) are taken from the *Amplified Bible,* Copyright 1954, 1958, 1962, 1964, 1965, 1987 by the Lockman Foundation. Used by permission.

Definitions marked *Strong's* are from *The New Strong's Expanded Exhaustive Concordance of the Bible,* Thomas Nelson Publishers, Inc. Nashville, Tennessee.

Definitions marked *Webster's* are from *Merriam-Webster's Online Dictionary,* http://www.m-w.com/dictionary

All rights reserved. No part of this book may be reproduced in any form without permission in writing from the publisher, except in the case of brief quotations embodied in church related publications, critical articles or reviews.

© Copyright 2015 Gena Matthews

Introduction

Kingdom Curriculum for Kids was written for the purpose of capturing the generation of youth that has not been indoctrinated with either a worldly or religious mindset and teaching them Kingdom principles in a way they can comprehend and understand.

Matthew 13:19

> *"When any one hears the word of the Kingdom, and understands it not, then comes the wicked one, and catches away that which was sown in his heart..."*

Table of Contents

Lesson 13……..The Purpose of the Kingdom

Lesson 14……..The Purpose of the Kingdom Pt.2

Lesson 15……..The Garden

Lesson 16……..The Garden Pt.2

Lesson 17……..The Garden Pt.3

Lesson 18……..Kingdom Cultivation

Lesson 19……..Cultivate

Lesson 20……..Colonization

Lesson 21……..Culture of Heaven

Lesson 22……..The Kingdom Has Come

Lesson 23……..Spiritual Sons

Lesson 24……..From Sons to Servants

Kingdom Curriculum for Kids

Lesson 13   The Purpose of the Kingdom

- Every king must have territory that he rules.

- A king without territory has no kingdom.

- Every king wants to expand or spread his influence and territory.

- Since God is King of kings, He wants to expand too.

- *Psalms 24:7-10* - God is the "King of Glory".

- The word "glory" is talking about God's "heavenly kingdom".

- God has filled all there is in the "heavenly kingdom".

- God had to create an "earthly kingdom" to expand His territory.

- God created the "earthly kingdom" by speaking it into existence.

- God's word is how He creates and upholds His Kingdom.

    - *John 1:1-3*
    - *Colossians 1:16-17*
    - *Hebrews 1:3*
    - *Hebrews 11:3*

Questions for Lesson 13

1. What does a king have to have to rule?

　
　
　

2. What happens to a king without territory?

　
　
　

3. What does every king want to do?

　
　
　

4. What does God want to do?

5. Who is God?

_____
_____
_____

6. What is the word "glory" talking about?

_____
_____
_____

7. What has God already filled?

_____
_____
_____

8. Why did God create an "earthly kingdom"?

_____
_____
_____

9. How did God create the "earthly kingdom"?

_____
_____
_____

10. How does God create and uphold His kingdom?

_____

_____

_____

Lesson 13   Kingdom Word Search

```
K I N G O F G L O R Y H I J T K L M
I A N S I H N G P U R P O S E C Y E
N B T F J K I F E D E C B A R Z X X
G U V U L R K S T U V L M E R N W I
O C P W F U G I Q N E M A A I O G S
I D X H Q R E S N O P T E R T P N T
K E Z Y O S E N Q G E X W T O Q I E
I F W J I L F X C L D Y V H R Y K N
N G T K V G D C P E A O U L Y C A C
G L O R Y H E S Q A B Z M Y D B E E
S P R E A D X D Y L N E V A E H P V
T S R Q P O N H K J I D L M Z A S U
H I J K L M N O P Q R G F E D C B A
```

CREATE	HEAVENLY	PURPOSE
EARTHLY	INFLUENCE	RULES
EVERY	KING	SPEAKING
EXISTENCE	KINGDOM	SPREAD
EXPAND	KING OF KINGS	TERRITORY
GLORY	KING OF GLORY	UPHOLDS

Kingdom Curriculum for Kids

Lesson 14   The Purpose of the Kingdom Pt. 2

- God desires to reproduce His Kingdom in the earth.

- To understand why God desires to do this, we must understand the nature of a king.

- A king's kingdom is a reflection of himself.

- You can tell what type of king you have by looking at his kingdom.

- We must look at the environment and conditions of a kingdom provided by the king for his citizens.

- This tells us about the king's character and what his will is for his kingdom.

Questions for Lesson 14

1. What does God desire to do?

_____
_____
_____

2. What do we have to understand in order to understand God's desire?

_____
_____
_____

3. What is a king's kingdom?

_____
_____
_____

4. How can you tell what type of king you have?

_____
_____
_____

5. What are the two things we must look at that a king provides for his citizens?

_____
_____
_____

6. What do these two things tell us about a king?

_____
_____
_____

Lesson 14   Good King Bad King Game

Split the students into two teams.

- Ask each team a question regarding a king and his kingdom either good or bad.

- The students will each have a turn just like a spelling bee.

- The first student to answer correctly, good or bad, receives a point.

- The team with the most points wins.

Kingdom Curriculum for Kids

Lesson 15   The Garden

- The earth was the place or domain where God decided to reproduce His Heavenly Kingdom.

- God spent 5 days filling it and making it suitable for the arrival of its first citizens.

- When everything was full and in place, God created Himself a Son, which would govern and rule His Kingdom in His stead.

- The Kingdom God delivered to man was an abundant, fruitful, full and overflowing one.

- The place in which God placed His son was called Eden.

- The word Eden means luxury, dainty, delight, finery, to luxuriate and to delight oneself.

- The condition of a king's kingdom and his citizens are a direct reflection of the king himself.

Questions for Lesson 15

1. Where did God decide to reproduce His Heavenly Kingdom?
   _____
   _____
   _____

2. How long did God take making the earth suitable for its first citizens?
   _____
   _____
   _____

3. When did God create for Himself a son?
   _____
   _____
   _____

4. What would sons of God do in His stead?
   _____
   _____
   _____

5. What was the Kingdom God delivered to man like?

_____

_____

_____

6. Where did God place His son Adam?

_____

_____

_____

7. What does Eden mean?

_____

_____

_____

8. What is a direct reflection of the King Himself?

_____

_____

_____

Eden Alphabet Game

Step 1 You slap each leg one at a time, clap your hands, and snap your fingers one hand at a time. Repeat continuously while playing the game.

Step 2 While doing step 1, each player names something that was in the garden of Eden by using a letter in the alphabet in order, while keeping time with step 1.

    Ex. "Eden had apples"
          "Eden had berries"
          "Eden had carrots"
          "
          "
          "

Step 3 The players are out if they do not answer in time or answer correctly. The last player in wins.

Kingdom Curriculum for Kids

Lesson 16 The Garden Pt. 2

- **God placed Adam and Eve in a garden called Eden, not a desert.**

- **This choice of environment is representative of God's abundant nature.**

- **1 Kings 10:1-13 - We see an example of this environment in the story of the Queen of Sheba.**

- **The Queen of Sheba came to examine King Solomon and his kingdom.**

- **The Bible says that she fainted from seeing the splendor of his kingdom.**

- **The Queen of Sheba looked at the condition of his servants and cupbearers.**

- **God the King of Kings, was the Source of Solomon's favor and wealth.**

- **God caused Solomon to prosper above and beyond any other king.**

- **God's intent for mankind and His Kingdom is restoration in its fullness.**

- **We see this restoration in this abundant gardenlike environment established again in the following scripture:**

  - **Isaiah 55:1**
  - **Revelation 2:7**
  - **Revelation 22:2**

Questions for Lesson 16

1. Where did God not place Adam and Eve?

2. What is representative of God's abundant nature?

3. Who came to see King Solomon and his kingdom?

4. What happened when she came?

5. What did the Queen of Sheba look at?

6. Who was the source of Solomon's favor and wealth?

7. What did God cause Solomon to do?

8. What is God's intent for mankind and His Kingdom?

9. How is God's character demonstrated and confirmed?

Decoding Kingdom Scripture

"__ __ __   __ __ __ __ __ __   __ __ __   __ __ __ __ __   __
 1 14 4   6 15 18 13 5 4   21 19   9 14 20 15   1

__ __ __ __ __ __ __ (__   __ __ __ __ __   __ __ __ __ __).
11 9 14 7 4 15 13   1   18 15 25 1 12   18 1 3 5

__ __ __ __ __ __ __   __ __   __ __ __   __ __ __   __ __ __
16 18 9 5 19 20 19   20 15   8 9 13   7 15 4   1 14 4

__ __ __ __ __ __----__   __ __ __   __ __   __ __ __
6 1 20 8 5 18   20 15 8 9 13   2 5   20 8 5

__ __ __ __ __   __ __ __   __ __ __   __ __ __ __ __   __ __ __
7 12 15 18 25   1 14 4   20 8 5   16 15 23 5 18   1 14 4

__ __ __   __ __ __ __ __ __ __   __ __ __   __ __ __
20 8 5   13 1 10 5 19 20 25   1 14 4   20 8 5

__ __ __ __ __ __ __   __ __ __ __ __ __ __ __   __ __ __
4 15 13 9 14 15 14   20 8 18 15 21 7 8 15 21 20 20 8 5

__ __ __ __   __ __ __   __ __ __ __ __ __   __ __ __
1 7 5 19   1 14 4   6 15 18 5 22 5 18   1 14 4

__ __ __ __   __ __ __ __ __ (__ __   __ __   __ __)."
5 22 5 18   1 13 5 14   19 15   2 5   9 20

__ __ __ __ __ __ __ __ __   1:6   __ __ __
18 5 22 5 12 1 20 9 15 14   1 13 16

*Use the decoding key on next page.

Decoding Kingdom Scripture Answer Key

A	B	C	D	E	F	G	H	I	J	K	L	M	N	O	P	Q	R	S	T	U	V	W	X	Y	Z
1	2	3	4	5	6	7	8	9	10	11	12	13	14	15	16	17	18	19	20	21	22	23	24	25	26

Kingdom Curriculum for Kids

Lesson 17   The Garden Pt. 3

- The garden environment aspect of the Kingdom is often overlooked.

- We need to understand this aspect of the Kingdom to understand God's will for us.

- Many of the problems we face in our lives come from low expectations.

- People wrongly believe that God condones lack and poverty in the lives of His citizens.

- God's character is one of abundance.

- There is no lack or poverty in God's Heavenly Kingdom.

- God intended for His (earthly) physical Kingdom to reflect or look like His Heavenly Kingdom.

- **God is not stingy.**

- **He does not delight in the lack and poverty in the lives of His people.**

- **Just the opposite, Psalms 35:27 says, "Let the Lord be magnified, which hath pleasure in the prosperity of his servant."**

- **If the king's servants and citizens are prosperous, it is a direct reflection of the king's character.**

Questions for Lesson 17

1. What aspect of the Kingdom is often overlooked?
___
___
___

2. Why do we need to understand this aspect of the Kingdom?
___
___
___

3. Where do many of the problems we face in life come from?
___
___
___

4. What do people wrongly believe?
___
___
___

5. What is God's character like?

_____

_____

_____

6. What is not in God's Heavenly Kingdom?

_____

_____

_____

7. What did God intend for His earthly physical Kingdom to do?

_____

_____

_____

8. God is not what?

_____

_____

_____

9. What does God not delight in?

_____

_____

_____

10. What does God have pleasure in?

_____
_____
_____

11. What do the king's servants and citizen's prosperity reflect on?

_____
_____
_____

The Garden of Eden Word Scramble

1. esrte ___ ___ ___ ___ ___

2. salpnt ___ ___ ___ ___ ___ ___

3. ivrre ___ ___ ___ ___ ___

4. sniop ___ ___ ___ ___ ___

5. ngiho ___ ___ ___ ___ ___

6. dlehdiek ___ ___ ___ ___ ___ ___ ___ ___

7. tseepuhar ___ ___ ___ ___ ___ ___ ___ ___ ___

8. ldgo ___ ___ ___ ___

9. mbeludli ___ ___ ___ ___ ___ ___ ___ ___

10. xnoy ___ ___ ___ ___

Kingdom Curriculum for Kids

Lesson 18   Kingdom Cultivation

- **Genesis 2:15 "Then the Lord God took the man and put him into the garden of Eden to cultivate it and keep it."**

- **God desired to expand His Kingdom by creating a Kingdom that reflected His heavenly one.**

- **When God created His physical kingdom, He gave the right to rule this Kingdom to His representatives and sons-mankind.**

- **To facilitate this delegation of authority and rule, God created man in His "image" and "likeness".**

- **God created man to be a trinity; like Him.**

- **Man had a body, soul (mind) and spirit.**

- **Man was literally the reflection of God on earth.**

- **The earth was a reflection of its heavenly original.**

- Man was created a "human being", possessing a physical body.

- Man's physical body specifically qualified him to govern and rule over all that pertained to the earth.

- The word "human" comes from the word "humus" which means earth.

- Man is made of the same substance as the earth, but possesses the very spirit of God Himself as his life.

- Because of man's physical and spiritual characteristics, man had the ability to operate in the spiritual realm as well as the physical (earth) realm, under the direction of God.

Questions for Lesson 18

1. What was man responsible for doing in the garden?

___

2. What did God desire to do?

___

3. Who did God give the right to rule this earthly kingdom to?

___

4. How did God facilitate this delegation of authority and rule?

___

5. How did God create man like Him?
_____
_____
_____

6. What did man have?
_____
_____
_____

7. What was man?
_____
_____
_____

8. What was the earth?
_____
_____
_____

9. What did man possess?
_____
_____
_____

10. What did the physical body specifically qualify man for?
___
___
___

11. Where does the word "human" come from and what does it mean?
___
___
___

12. What did man have the ability to do?
___
___
___

Lesson 18 Kingdom Search Word Puzzle

```
O N H E Y T O J L A U T I R I P S
M S E V I T A T N E S E R P E R P
L A J D X S N I G Y I N E V A E H
K U H T R A E T A T I L I C A F Y
D T G O V E R N F S U M U H D L S
E H I C G R M M T R I N I T Y E I
I O G A W N O I T A V I T L U C C
F R M B Y D E L E G A T I O N T A
I I F A G Q L S S E N E K I L E L
L T Z N U P K H E C R E A T E D B
A Y I L A N I G I R O P E R A T E
U K P E R T A I N E D C M L A E R
Q C H A R A C T E R I S T I C S A
```

KINGDOM   LIKENESS   RULE
CULTIVATION   TRINITY   CREATED
REFLECTED   ORIGINAL   IMAGE
HEAVENLY   QUALIFIED   SPIRITUAL
PHYSICAL   GOVERN   REALM
REPRESENTATIVES PERTAINED   CHARACTERISTICS
FACILITATE   HUMUS   AUTHORITY
DELEGATION   EARTH   OPERATE

Kingdom Curriculum for Kids

Lesson 19   Cultivate

- Genesis 2:15 "Then the Lord God took the man and put him into the garden of Eden to cultivate it and keep it."

- God created and established man as His representative.

- He gave him the assignment to keep and recreate the culture of God's heavenly kingdom, in His physical kingdom, here in the earth.

- Adam's original job description was to "cultivate" (to dress and keep).

- God intended for Adam and his seed to spread this Garden until it filled the entire earth.

- Webster defines the word "cultivate" as, "fostering growth and improvement".

- The word "culture" and "cultivate" come from the same root.

- The word "culture" is the practices, ways, custom, laws and social norms of a people, nation or kingdom.

- The Latin root word from which we get the word "cultivate" is "colere".

- This is the same root word from which we get the word "colony".

- Webster defines a "colony" as: *"a body of people living in a new territory but retaining ties with its parent state.*

- These ties are generally characterized by "governmental control", and the "preservation of the parent nation's culture".

Questions for Lesson 19

1. What did God do with man?

   _____
   _____
   _____

2. What assignment did God give man?

   _____
   _____
   _____

3. What was Adam's original job description?

   _____
   _____
   _____

4. What did God intend for Adam and his seed?

   _____
   _____
   _____

5. What does the word "cultivate" mean?

6. What does the word "culture" mean?

7. What is the Latin word for "cultivate"?

8. What word comes from that same root word?

9. What is a colony?

10. The ties retained with the parent state are generally characterized by what?

_____

_____

_____

Lesson 19   Cultivate Word Game

How many words can you make up from the word <u>cultivate</u>? The person with the most words wins.

_____
_____
_____
_____
_____
_____
_____
_____
_____
_____
_____
_____
_____
_____
_____
_____
_____
_____

 # Kingdom Curriculum for Kids

Lesson 20   Colonization

- **Colonization is the process of establishing a colony with the culture, laws and customs of the parent nation.**

- **A colony's primary purpose is to convert and transform the inhabitants and the territory being colonized to reflect the parent country.**

- **God's command of cultivation was really one of "colonization".**

- **Adam was to colonize the earth with the practices, ways and social norms of the culture of heaven.**

- **This would cause God's kingdom and will to be done on earth as it is in heaven.**

- **God's command to Adam to "cultivate" the Garden, was really a "Kingdom expansion strategy".**

- **Adam was to cultivate a territory and reproduce the parent country's culture in another location, thereby expanding God's Kingdom.**

- **Adam's job was not simply that of a gardener, but an ambassador and governor.**

- **Adam was responsible for developing and establishing the Kingdom of Heaven's culture in its physical outpost or colony called earth.**

Questions for Lesson 20

1. What is colonization?

2. What is a colony's primary purpose?

3. What was God's command of cultivation like?

4. What was Adam supposed to do?

5. What would be done on the earth as it is in heaven?

_____
_____
_____

6. What was God's command to Adam really?

_____
_____
_____

7. What was Adam's job?

_____
_____
_____

8. What was Adam responsible for?

_____
_____
_____

Colonization Word Puzzle

Follow the directions below to transform the word <u>colonization</u> to the word <u>kingdom</u>.

1. Take the word <u>colonization</u> and switch the letters i and n.
2. Take the letters and switch the letter n to m.
3. Take the letters and remove the second letter i.
4. Take the letters and switch the letter z to g.
5. Take the letters and replace the letters a and t with the letter d.
6. Take the letters and remove the second o.
7. Take the letters and remove the letters col and replace them with the letter k.

_____

_____

_____

_____

_____

_____

_____

Kingdom Curriculum for Kids

Lesson 21   Culture of Heaven

The picture of what the culture of the Kingdom of Heaven looked like in a physical kingdom is in Genesis chapters 1 and 2.

In Genesis chapters 1 and 2 there was no:
1. Sin
2. Death
3. Sickness
4. Fear
5. Lack and insufficiency
6. Sweating, toiling or laboring
7. Need for deliverance from demon possession or otherwise

This was the culture God intended for His earthly Kingdom to possess.

- When man sinned, he died spiritually and started the process of physical "death" and "sickness".

- When the Kingdom was removed, man experienced fear for the first time.

- Man declared to God, "I was afraid".

- Man realized that he was naked and in need. (lack and insufficiency)

- Man now had to sweat, toil and labor in sorrow to have his needs met.

- Mankind's authority in the earth was transferred to Satan.

- Man now had to avoid becoming a victim to the enemy's attempts to possess and bind him.

- Man now needed "deliverance".

Questions for Lesson 21

1. Where can we find a picture of what the culture of the Kingdom of Heaven looked like?

   _____
   _____
   _____

2. What seven things were not in the culture of Heaven?

   _____
   _____
   _____

3. What happened when men sinned?

   _____
   _____
   _____

4. What happened when the Kingdom was removed?

   _____
   _____
   _____

5. What did man declare to God?

_____
_____
_____

6. What did man realize?

_____
_____
_____

7. What did man have to do to have his needs met?

_____
_____
_____

8. What happened to mankind's authority?

_____
_____
_____

9. What did man now have to avoid?

_____
_____
_____

10. What did man need?
___
___
___

Culture of Heaven Search Word Puzzle

```
Y T I R E P S O R P J I Y P Q E
C O B E S E X Y Z O K H X O P D
N A J P L A B O R W L G W N E C
E C D O T C E I A E F F K M E B
I N V R H E L M B R M E C L K A
C E F I L T N A D N U B A K D S
I L I O T H A N C U N E L R N S
F H M A S G O E D V O D V J A E
F L E Q U F P Q D W P C U I S N
U W K O V B K J E X Q B T H S K
S I N I W A C D F Y R A S G E C
N O I S I V O R P T S Z R F R I
I F G J E C N A R E V I L E D S
```

ABUNDANT – LIFE	PROSPERITY	DELIVERANCE
JOY	PEACE	LOVE
PROVISION	POWER	DRESS – AND – KEEP
SIN	SICKNESS	DEATH
FEAR	LACK	INSUFFICIENCY
SWEAT	TOIL	LABOR

Kingdom Curriculum for Kids

Lesson 22   The Kingdom Has Come

- **Jesus not only came to save our souls, but to reestablish man's access to the Kingdom of Heaven in the earth.**

- **John the Baptist and Jesus Himself both announced that the Kingdom of God has come.**

- **As proof of the presence of the Kingdom, Jesus spoke of men having present access to it by repenting of their sins and being born again of the Spirit.**

- **Wherever the Gospel of the Kingdom was preached, the culture of heaven was restored.**

- **Jesus would often enter into a city and proclaim the Gospel of the Kingdom (the presence of the Kingdom in their midst).**

The following results of the loss of the Kingdom were restored:
1. People repented of sin. (Matthew 4:23, 9:35, 15:32-38)
2. People were raised from the dead. (Luke 7:11-14)
3. People were healed of all manner of infirmity and sickness. (Matthew 4:23, 9:35, 15:32-38)
4. People were commanded not to worry or be afraid because of the Kingdom. (Matthew 6:32-33)
5. Lack and insufficiency were met with abundance and sufficiency. (Matthew 14:15-21, 15:32-38)
6. People received not through toil and labor, but through seeking the Kingdom of God first. (Matthew 6:33)
7. People were delivered from demonic possession and given authority over all the power of the enemy. (Matthew 12:28, Luke 10:19)

Because of Jesus' finished work on the cross and becoming a curse for us, He has effectively made available to us the culture and conditions found in the Garden of Eden.

Because of the presence of the kingdom of darkness, we must reclaim territory for the Kingdom of God and grow its influence throughout the earth.

Questions for Lesson 22

1. What did Jesus come to do outside of save our souls?

_____
_____
_____

2. What did Jesus and John the Baptist both do?

_____
_____
_____

3. How did men have access to the Kingdom of God?

_____
_____
_____

4. What happened wherever the gospel of the Kingdom was preached?

_____
_____
_____

5. What would Jesus do when He entered a city?

_____
_____
_____

6. What seven things happened when the Kingdom was restored?

_____
_____
_____

7. What happened because of Jesus' finished work on the cross and His becoming a curse for us?

_____
_____
_____

8. Why do we have to reclaim territory for the Kingdom of God?

_____
_____
_____

Lesson 22   Decode Kingdom Scripture

A B C D E F G H I J K L M N O P Q R S T
1 2 3 4 5 6 7 8 9 10 11 12 13 14 15 16 17 18 19 20

U V W X Y Z 6 3
21 22 23 24 25 26 27 28

__ __ __ __ __ __ __ __:__ __ __ "__ __ __ __ __ __ __
13 1 20 20 8 5 23   27 28 28   2 21 20   19 5 5 11

__ __ __ __ __ __ __ __ __ __ __ __ __ __ __ __ __ __
25 5   6 9   18 19 20   20 8 5   11 9 14 7 4 15 13

__ __ __ __ __ __, __ __ __ __ __ __
15 6   7 15 4   1 14 4   8 9 19

__ __ __ __ __ __ __ __ __ __ __ __ __: __ __ __
18 9 7 8 20 5 15 21 19 14 5 19 19   1 14 4

__ __ __ __ __ __ __ __ __ __ __ __ __ __ __
 1 12 12   20 8 5 19 5   20 8 9 14 7 19

__ __ __ __ __ __ __ __ __ __ __ __ __ __ __
19 8 1 12 12   2 5   1 4 4 5 4   21 14 20 15

__ __ __."
25 15 21

Kingdom Curriculum for Kids

Lesson 23   Spiritual Sons

- **In Genesis 1:26-28, when God created His physical kingdom, he did not set angels to rule over it, but men.**

- **God made human beings that possessed his nature, image and likeness.**

- **God gave man the ability to transact or communicate between the spiritual and the natural worlds.**

- **Man had such a likeness to God that he was called the "son of God" (Luke 3:38).**

- **This "kingdom of sons" was to rule this physical kingdom on God's behalf forever.**

- **God's original plan for mankind was that he would never die nor have to leave the earth to experience heaven.**

- **Heaven was to be on earth (Revelation 21 & 22).**

Questions for Lesson 23

1. Who did God set to rule over the earth?

   _____
   _____

2. What three things did human beings possess that made them like God?

   _____
   _____
   _____

3. What was mankind called in Luke 3:38?

   _____

4. How long did God originally plan for the "kingdom of sons" to rule this physically kingdom?

   _____

5. What was God's original plan for mankind?

   _____
   _____

6. Where was heaven supposed to be experienced?

   _____

Lesson 23   Arts and Crafts

Ask the children to imagine what they think heaven would look like and then ask them to draw it.

Use color pencils or crayons.

Kingdom Curriculum for Kids

Lesson 24   From Sons to Servants

- **The loss of the Kingdom of God had large impact on mankind.**

- **The sin of man was more than an act of disobedience.**

- **The sin of man was an act of treason and a declaration of independence from the government of God.**

- **Man's loss of the kingdom altered his relationship with God.**

- **Man's loss of the kingdom altered the earth and the way man got his needs met.**

- **When Adam sinned, he spiritually died. Genesis 2:16-17**

- **Adam physically lived for 930 years.**

- **But when Adam ate the forbidden fruit, he spiritually died immediately.**

- Adam and Eve's bodies began the process of expiring from the moment they sinned.

Let's look at the example of a fish.

- If you take a fish out of water or the natural environment of the fish, it will not die immediately.

- The process of expiring happens because the fish is out of its environment.

- When Adam and Eve sinned, they were taken out of the environment of the Kingdom of God and God's presence.

- When this occurred, Adam was no longer a son of God, but a servant to the world he was created to rule. Genesis 3:17-19.

- Because of Adam's sin, every human being is born into the world with sin and spiritually dead, expiring and having to care for themselves.

- This is why everyone must be born again of the Spirit of God, so that we can once again enter the Kingdom of God.

Questions for Lesson 24

1. What had a large impact on mankind?

   _____
   _____

2. What was the sin of man considered?

   _____
   _____
   _____

3. What three things were altered when man lost the Kingdom of God?

   _____
   _____
   _____

4. What happened to Adam when he sinned?

   _____
   _____

5. How long did Adam live physically?

　　_____

6. What happens when we are taken out of our natural environment?

　　_____
　　_____
　　_____

7. What did Adam become when he lost his sonship?

　　_____

8. How do all human beings come into the world?

　　_____
　　_____
　　_____

9. What has to happen for human beings to regain entrance into the Kingdom of God?

　　_____
　　_____
　　_____

Lesson 24 Sons or Servants Word Scramble

Unscramble the following words which describe the difference between sons and servants.

1. itarlipus   ___ ___ ___ ___ ___ ___ ___ ___ ___
2. lanutar   ___ ___ ___ ___ ___ ___ ___
3. grine   ___ ___ ___ ___ ___
4. veres   ___ ___ ___ ___ ___
5. erlu   ___ ___ ___ ___
6. lito   ___ ___ ___ ___
7. arelten   ___ ___ ___ ___ ___ ___ ___
8. xeerip   ___ ___ ___ ___ ___ ___
9. nisbsegls   ___ ___ ___ ___ ___ ___ ___ ___
10. sucer   ___ ___ ___ ___ ___
11. pinhoss   ___ ___ ___ ___ ___ ___ ___
12. dotnreohvas ___ ___ ___ ___ ___ ___ ___ ___ ___ ___

Answer Key

Lesson 13 Kingdom Word Search

```
K I N G O F G L O R Y H I J T K L M
I A N S I H N G P U R P O S E C Y E
N B T F J K I F E D E C B A R Z X X
G U V U L R K S T U V L M E R N W I
O C P W F U G I Q N E M A A I O G S
F D X H Q R E S N O P T E R T P N T
K E Z Y O S E N Q G E X W T O Q I E
I F W J I L F X C L D Y V H R Y K N
N G T K U G D C P E A O U L Y C A C
G L O R Y H E S Q A B Z M Y D B E E
S P R E A D X D Y L N E V A E H P V
T S R Q P O N H K J I D L M Z A S U
H I J K L M N O P Q R G F E D C B A
```

CREATE	HEAVENLY	PURPOSE
EARTHLY	INFLUENCE	RULES
EVERY	KING	SPEAKING
EXISTENCE	KINGDOM	SPREAD
EXPAND	KING OF KINGS	TERRITORY
GLORY	KING OF GLORY	UPHOLDS

Answer Key

Lesson 17   The Garden of Eden Word Scramble

1. esrte   trees
2. salpnt   plants
3. ivrre   river
4. sniop   Pison
5. ngiho   Gihon
6. dlehdiek   Hiddekel
7. tseepuhar   Euphrates
8. ldgo   gold
9. mbeludli   bdellium
10. xnoy   onyx

Answer Key

Lesson 18 Kingdom Search Word Puzzle

```
O N H E Y T O J L A U T I R I P S
M S E V I T A T N E S E R P E R P
L A J D X S N I G Y L N E V A E H
K U H T R A E T A T I L I C A F Y
D T G O V E R N F S U M U H D L S
E H I C G R M M T R I N I T Y E I
I O G A W N O I T A V I T L U C C
F R M B Y D E L E G A T I O N T A
I I F A G Q L S S E N E K I L E L
L T Z N U P K H E C R E A T E D B
A Y I L A N I G I R O P E R A T E
U K P E R T A I N E D C M L A E R
Q C H A R A C T E R I S T I C S A
```

KINGDOM	LIKENESS	AUTHORITY
CULTIVATION	TRINITY	RULE
REFLECTED	ORIGINAL	CREATED
HEAVENLY	QUALIFIED	IMAGE
PHYSICAL	GOVERN	OPERATE
REPRESENTATIVES	PERTAINED	SPIRITUAL
FACILITATE	HUMUS	REALM
DELEGATION	EARTH	CHARACTERISTICS

Answer Key

Lesson 20   Colonization Word Puzzle

1. c o l o i n z a t i o n
2. c o l o i n z a t i o m
3. c o l o i n z a t o m
4. c o l o i n g a t o m
5. c o l o i n g d o m
6. c o l i n g d o m
7. k i n g d o m

Answer Key

Lesson 21   Culture of Heaven Search Word Puzzle

```
Y T I R E P S O R P J I Y P Q E
C O B E S E X Y Z O K H X O P D
N A J P L A B O R W L G W N E C
E C D O T C E R A E F F K M E B
I N V R H E L M B R M E C L K A
C E F I L T N A D N U B A K D S
I L I O T H A N C U N E L R N S
F H M A S G O E D V O D V J A E
F L E Q U F P Q D W P C U I S N
U W K O V B K J E X Q B T H S K
S I N I W A C D F Y R A S G E C
N O I S I V O R P T S Z R F R I
I F G J E C N A R E V I L E D S
```

ABUNDANT-LIFE	PROSPERITY	DELIVERANCE
JOY	PEACE	LOVE
PROVISION	POWER	DRESS-AND-KEEP
SIN	SICKNESS	DEATH
FEAR	LACK	INSUFFICIENCY
SWEAT	TOIL	LABOR

# Answer Key

Lesson 22   Decode Kingdom Scripture

A B C D E F G H I J K L M N O P Q R S T U V W X Y Z
1 2 3 4 5 6 7 8 9 10 11 12 13 14 15 16 17 18 19 20 21 22 23 24 25 26

6 3
27 28

M A T T H E W   6 : 3 3
13 1 20 20 8 5 23   27 28 28

"B U T   S E E K   Y E   F I R S T   T H E   K I N G D O M   O F
2 21 20   19 5 5 11   25 5   6 9 18 19 20   20 8 5   11 9 14 7 4 15 13   15 6

G O D,   A N D   H I S   R I G H T E O U S N E S S: A N D   A L L
7 15 4   1 14 4   8 9 19   18 9 7 8 20 5 15 21 19 14 5 19 19   1 14 4   1 12 12

T H E S E   T H I N G S   S H A L L   B E   A D D E D   U N T O   Y O U."
20 8 5 19 5   20 8 9 14 7 19   19 8 1 12 12   2 5   1 4 4 5 4   21 14 20 15   25 15 21

Answer Key

Lesson 24 **Sons and Servants Word Scramble**

1. itarlipus — s p i r i t u a l
2. lanutar — n a t u r a l
3. grine — r e i g n
4. veres — s e r v e
5. erlu — r u l e
6. lito — t o i l
7. arelten — e t e r n a l
8. xeerip — e x p i r e
9. nisbsegls — b l e s s i n g
10. sucer — c u r s e
11. pinhoss — s o n s h i p
12. dotnreohvas — s e r v a n t h o o d

Kingdom Curriculum for Kids was created to give children ages 6-12 the opportunity to learn about the Kingdom of God at a level that they can understand while still learning the same Kingdom principles that adults are being taught. If we take the opportunity to teach children who are forming a way of thinking now, they will not have as great a difficulty in transforming the way they think to line up with God's Word. We must understand the Kingdom of God to see God's Word manifested in our lives and the lives of our children.

For more information about additional Kingdom teaching resources, please visit:

- **Gena Matthews Ministries at:** www.genamatthews.com
- **J.C. Matthews Ministries at:** www.jcmatthews.org

Made in United States
Troutdale, OR
09/07/2023

12723266R00045